HAL•LEONARD
HARMONICA
PLAY•ALONG

FOLK/ROCK

VOL. 4

T0081532

Harmonica by Steve Cohen
Guitar by Mike DeRose
Bass, Keyboard, and Drums by Chris Kringel

ISBN 978-1-4234-2350-8

Visit Hal Leonard Online at
www.halleonard.com

HAL•LEONARD®
CORPORATION
7777 W. BLUEMOUND RD. P.O. BOX 13819
MILWAUKEE, WISCONSIN 53213

FOLK/ROCK

CONTENTS

HARMONICA NOTATION LEGEND

Harmonica music can be notated two different ways: on a *musical staff*, and in *tablature*.

THE MUSICAL STAFF shows pitches and rhythms and is divided by bar lines into measures. Pitches are named after the first seven letters of the alphabet.

TABLATURE graphically represents the harmonica music. Each note will be accompanied by a number, 1 through 10, indicating what hole you are to play. The arrow that follows indicates whether to blow or draw. (All examples are shown using a C diatonic harmonica.)

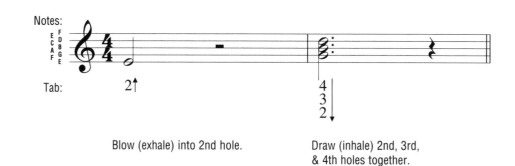

Blow (exhale) into 2nd hole.

Draw (inhale) 2nd, 3rd, & 4th holes together.

Notes on the C Harmonica

Exhaled (Blown) Notes

1	2	3	4	5	6	7	8	9	10
C	E	G	C	E	G	C	E	G	C

Inhaled (Drawn) Notes

1	2	3	4	5	6	7	8	9	10
D	G	B	D	F	A	B	D	F	A

Bends

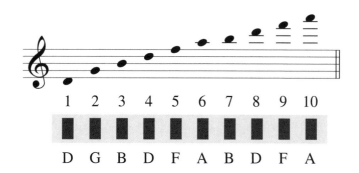

Blow Bends

- 1/4 step
- 1/2 step
- 1 step
- 1 1/2 steps

Draw Bends

- 1/4 step
- 1/2 step
- 1 step
- 1 1/2 steps

Definitions for Special Harmonica Notation

SLURRED BEND: Play (draw) 3rd hole, then bend the note down one whole step.

GRACE NOTE BEND: Starting with a pre-bent note, immediately release bend to the target note.

VIBRATO: Begin adding vibrato to the sustained note on beat 3.

TONGUE BLOCKING: Using your tongue to block holes 2 & 3, play octaves on holes 1 & 4.

NOTE: Tablature numbers in parentheses are used when:

- The note is sustained, but a new articulation begins (such as vibrato), or
- The quantity of notes being sustained changes, or
- A change in dynamics (volume) occurs.

Additional Musical Definitions

D.S. al Coda
- Go back to the sign (%), then play until the measure marked "*To Coda*," then skip to the section labelled "**Coda**."

D.C. al Fine
- Go back to the beginning of the song and play until the measure marked "*Fine*" (end).

- Repeat measures between signs.

(accent)
- Accentuate the note (play initial attack louder).

(staccato)
- Play the note short.

- When a repeated section has different endings, play the first ending only the first time and the second ending only the second time.

Dynamics

p
- Piano (soft)

mp
- Mezzo Piano (medium soft)

mf
- Mezzo Forte (medium loud)

f
- Forte (loud)

──────────── *(crescendo)*
- Gradually louder

──────────── *(decrescendo)*
- Gradually softer

Blowin' in the Wind

Words and Music by Bob Dylan

HARMONICA
Player: Bob Dylan
Harp Key: D Diatonic

*Chord symbols in parentheses are respective to guitar (Capo VII).

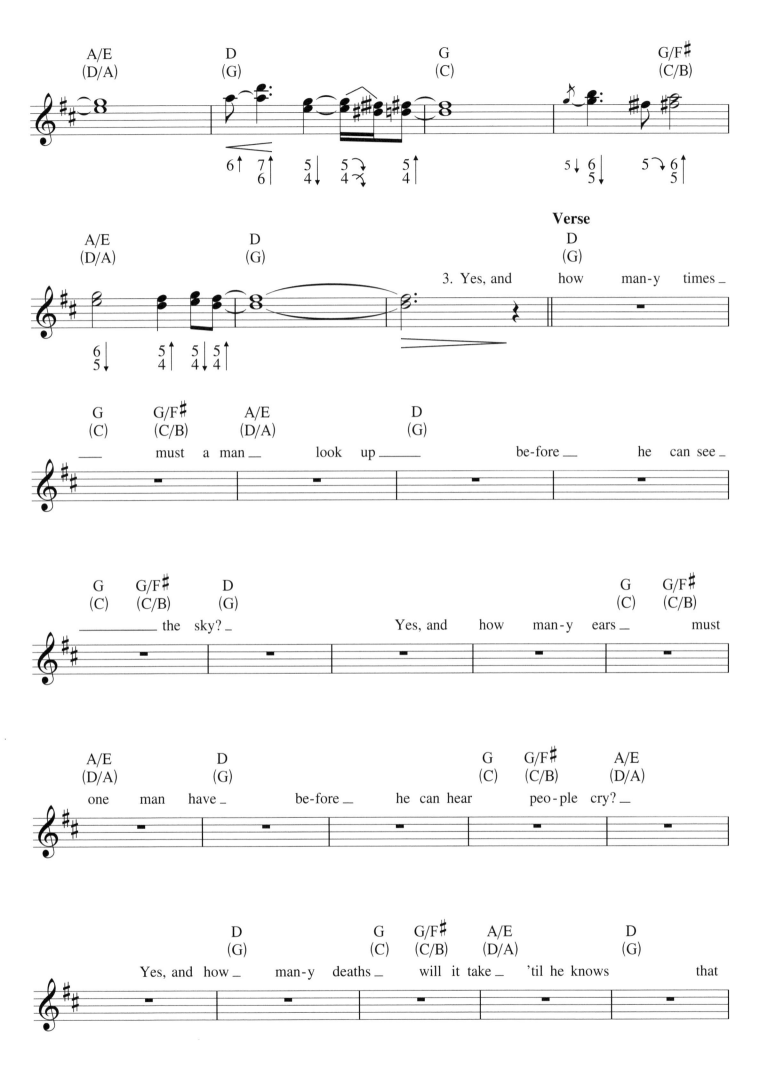

9

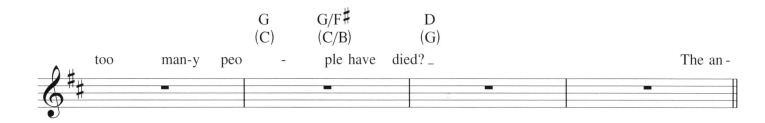

too man-y peo - ple have died? _ The an-

Chorus

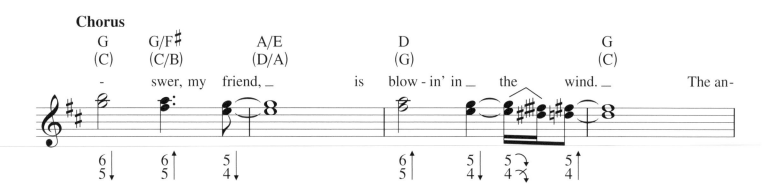

-swer, my friend, _ is blow-in' in _ the wind. _ The an-

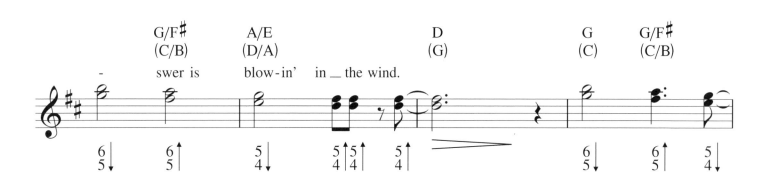

-swer is blow-in' in _ the wind.

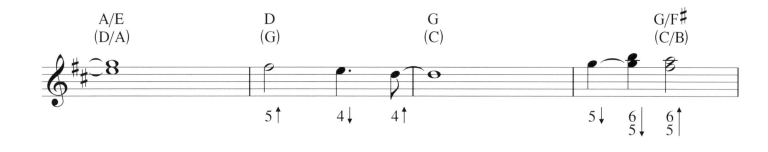

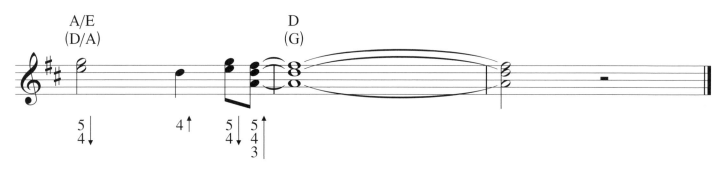

Catch the Wind

Words and Music by Donovan Leitch

H A R M O N I C A
Player: Donovan Leitch
Harp Key: E♭ Diatonic

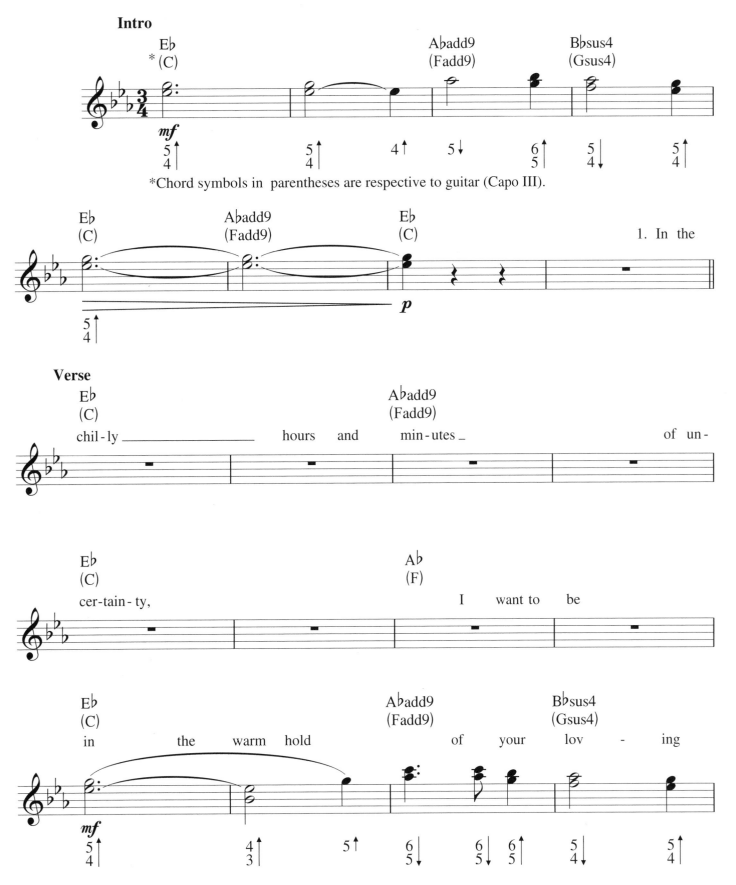

*Chord symbols in parentheses are respective to guitar (Capo III).

11

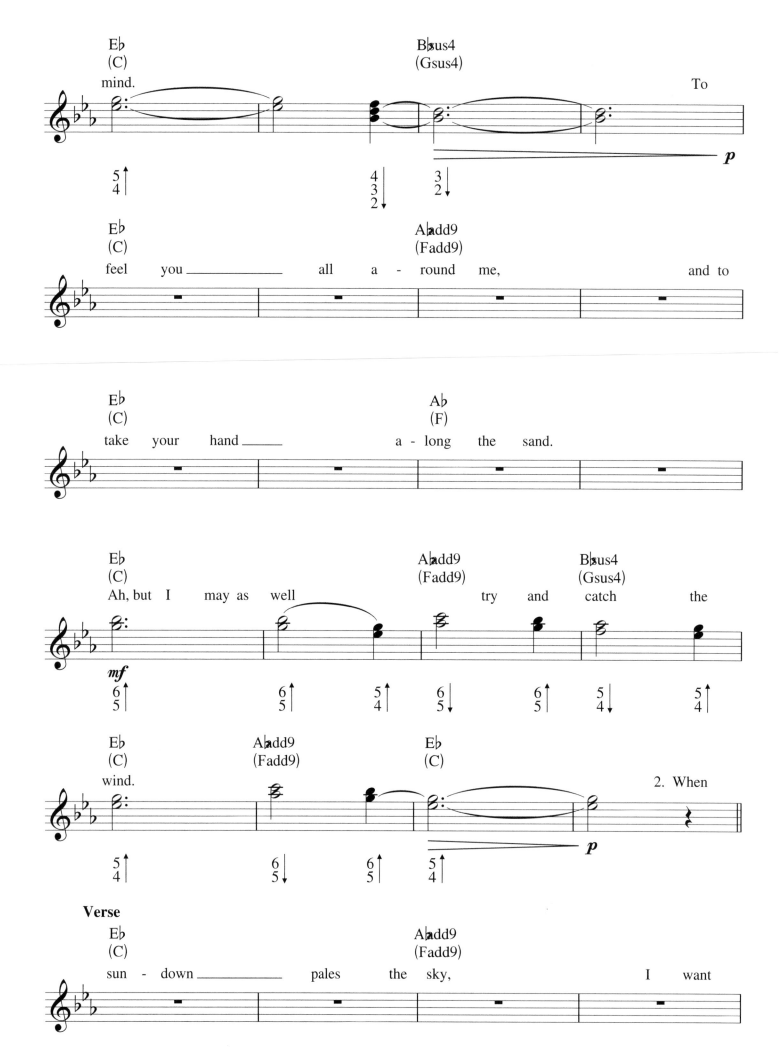

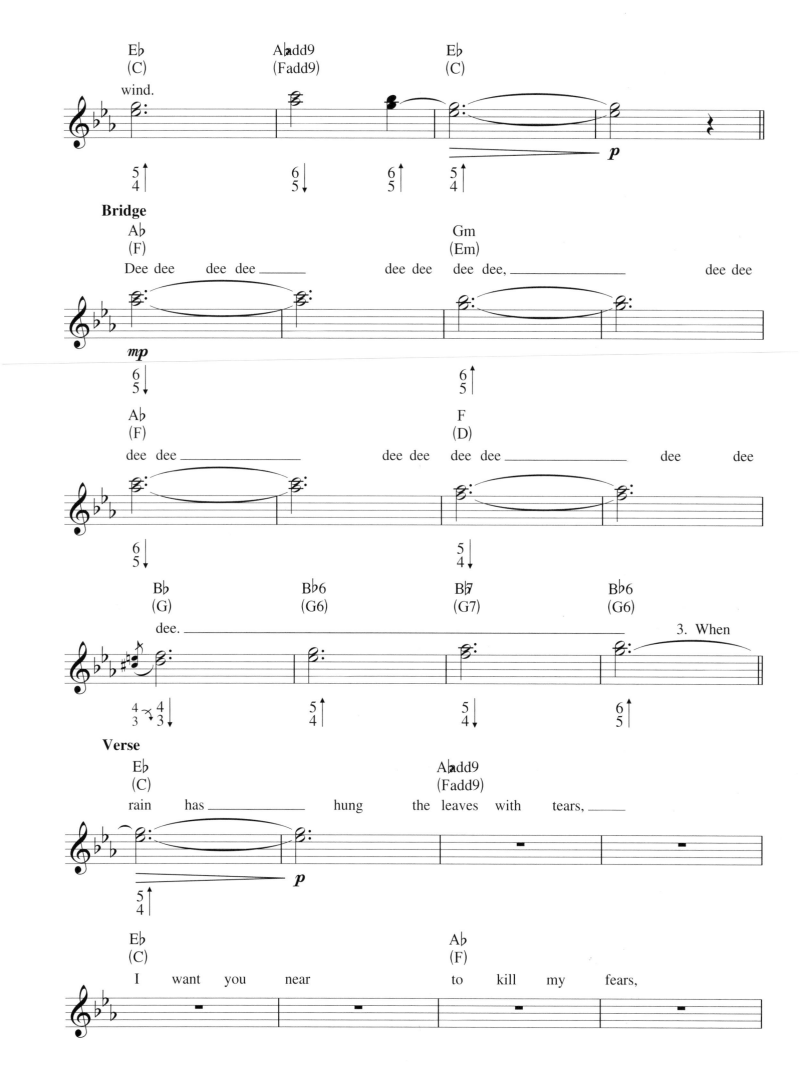

Interlude

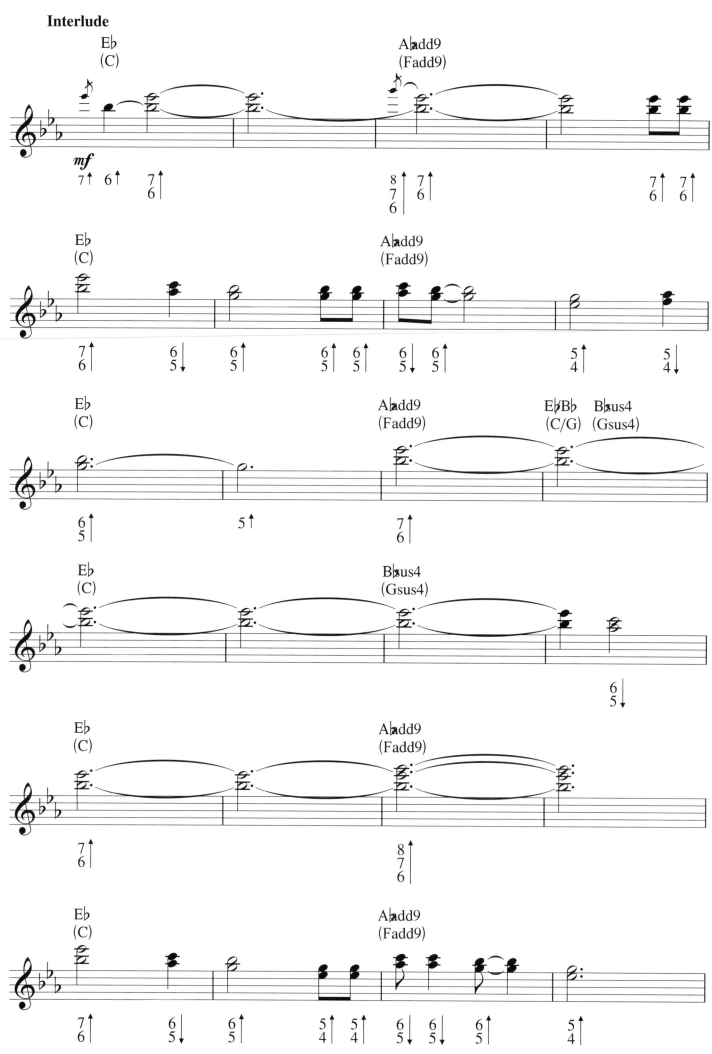

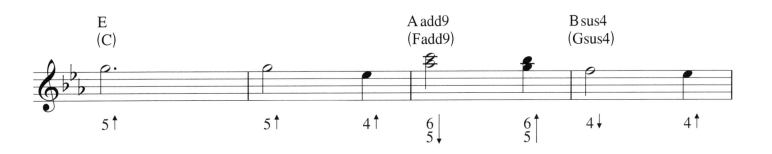

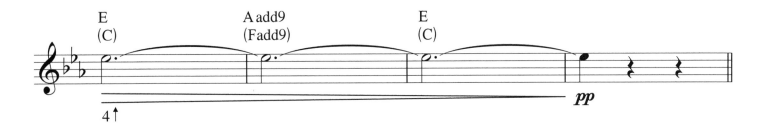

Outro-Guitar Solo

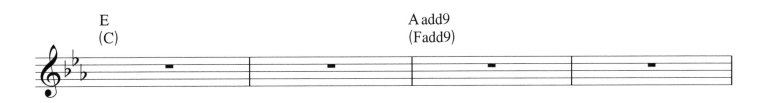

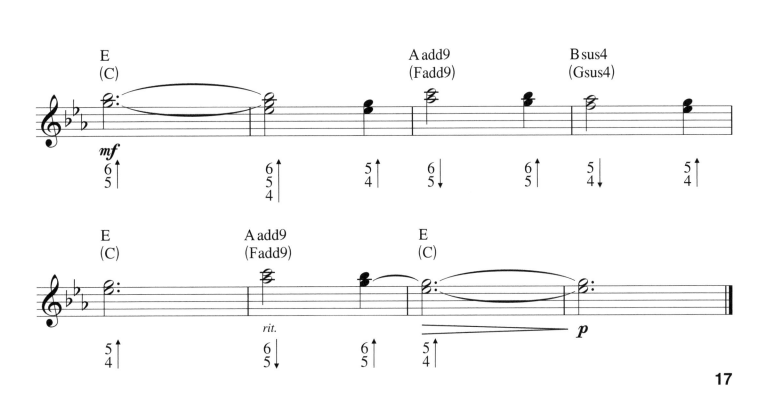

Daydream

Words and Music by John Sebastian

HARMONICA

Player: John Sebastian
Harp Keys: C Diatonic
　　　　　 D Diatonic
　　　　　 F Diatonic

18

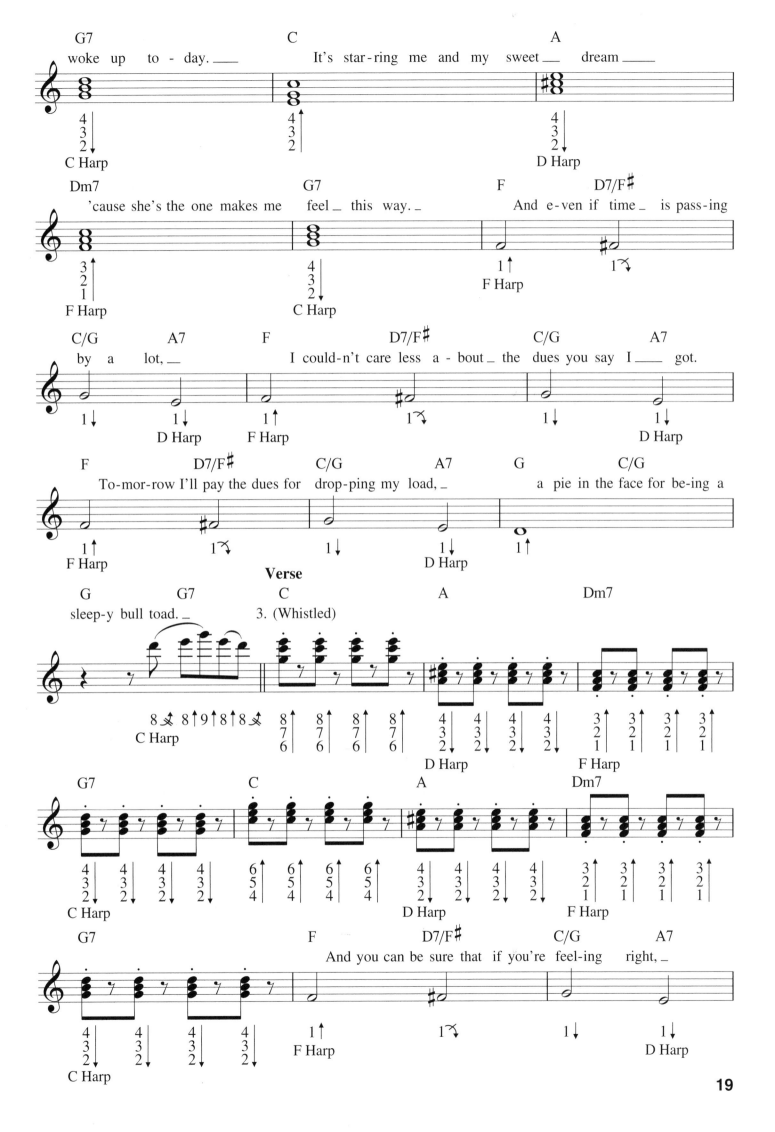

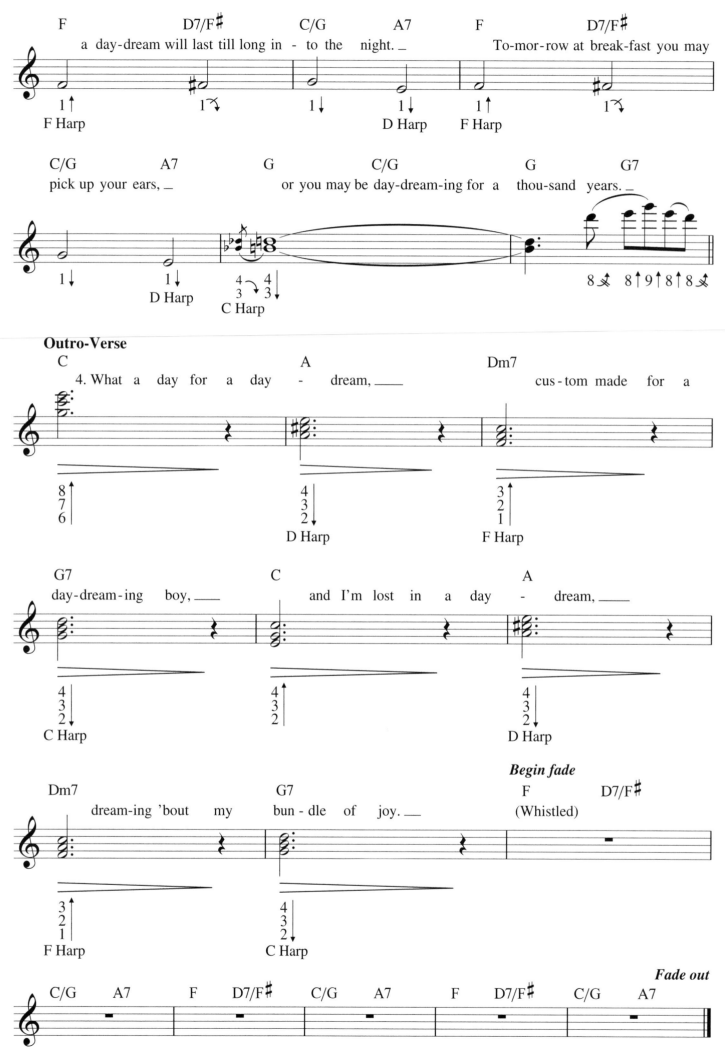

Eve of Destruction

Words and Music by P.F. Sloan and Steve Barri

H A R M O N I C A

Player: Anonymous
Harp Keys: G Diatonic
D Diatonic

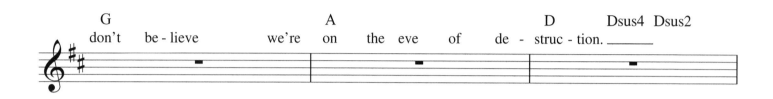

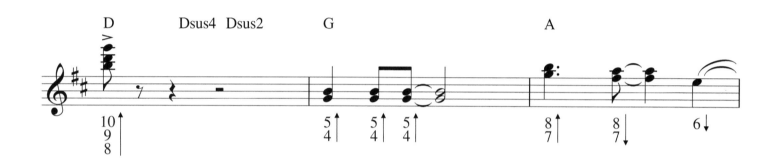

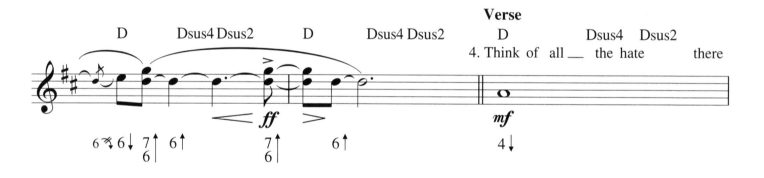

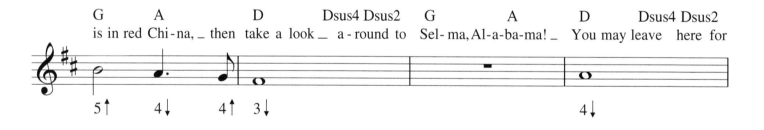

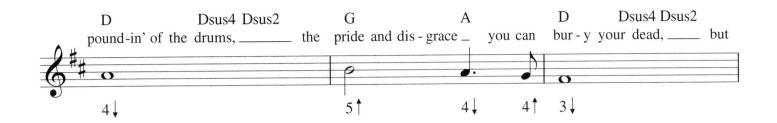

Chorus

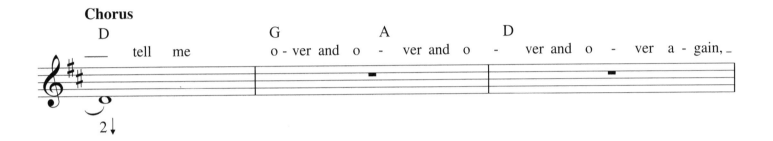

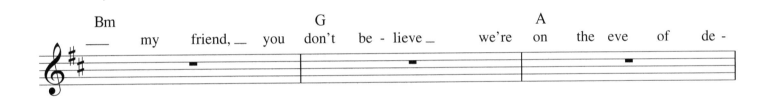

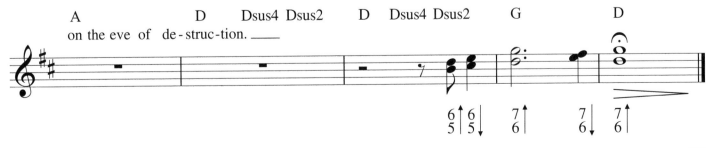

Mr. Tambourine Man

Words and Music by Bob Dylan

HARMONICA

Player: Bob Dylan
Harp Key: F Diatonic

*Chord symbols in parentheses are respective to guitar (Drop D tuning, Capo III).

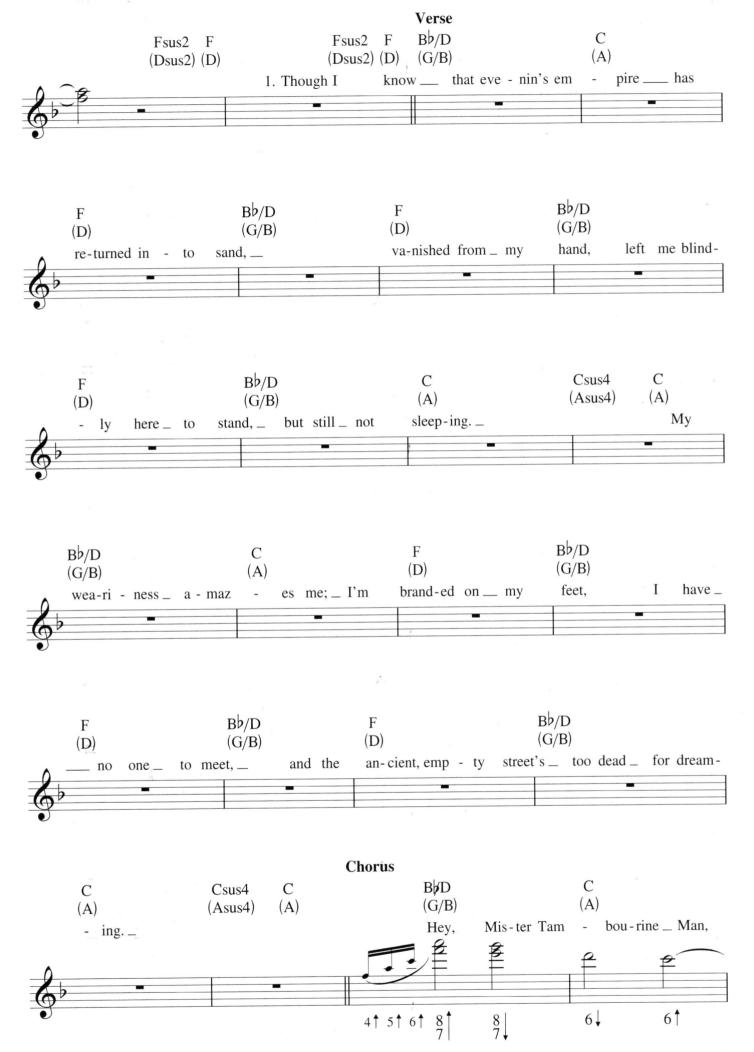

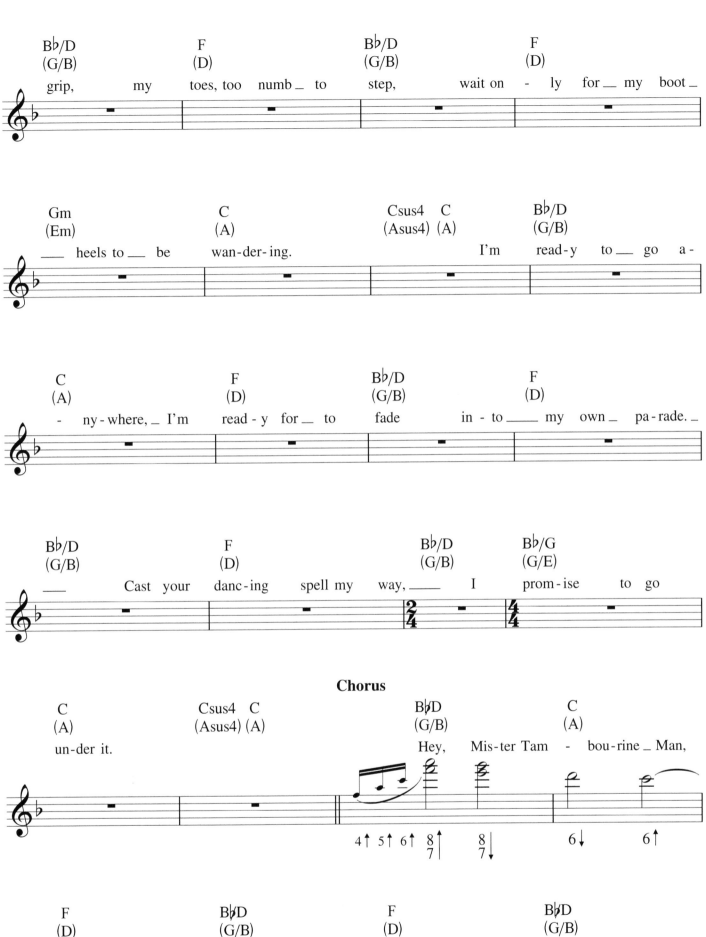

Chorus

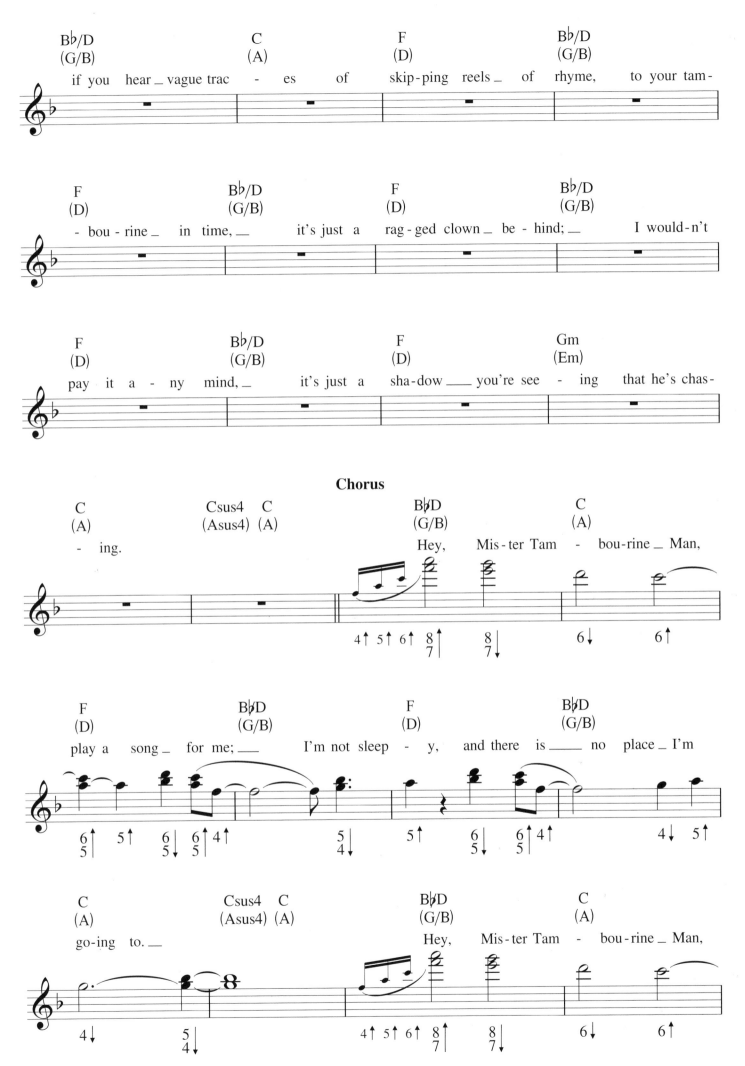

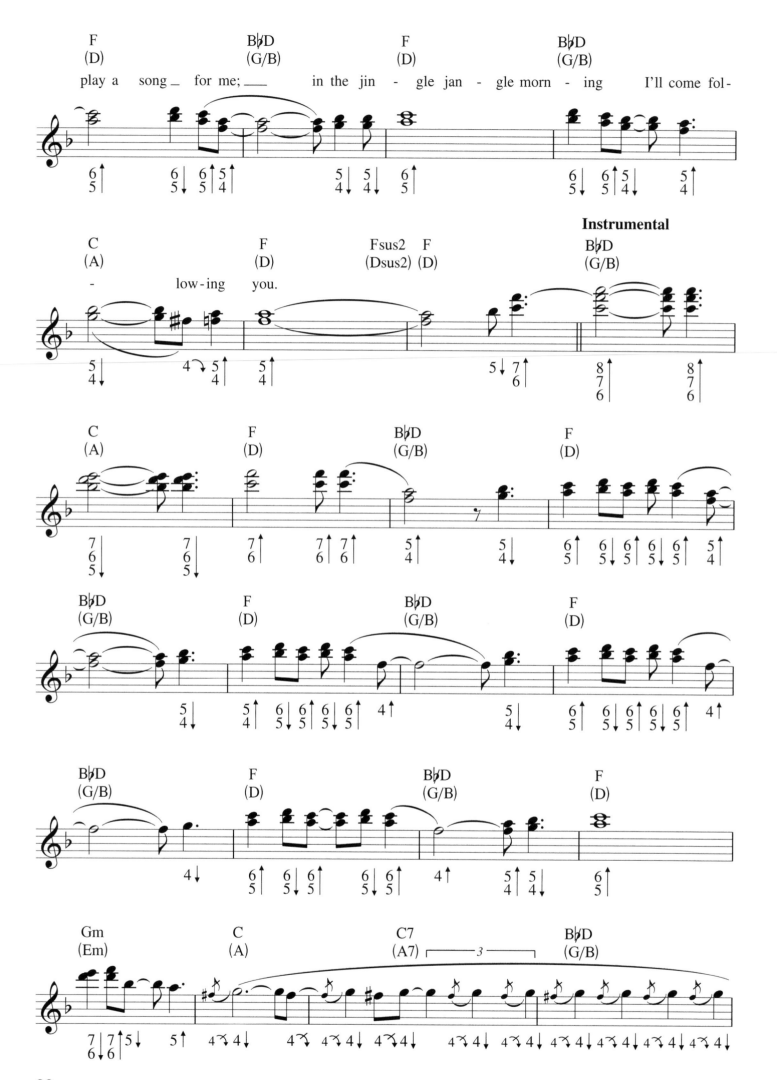

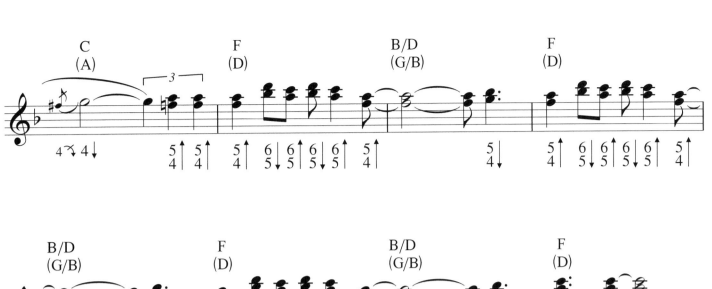

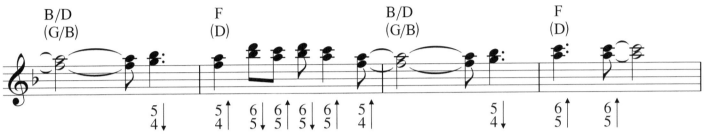

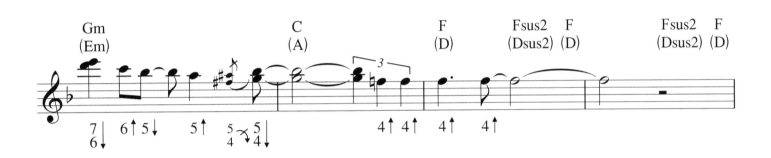

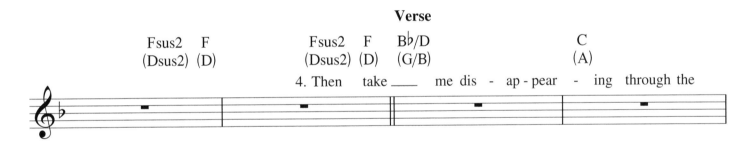

Verse

Fsus2   F   Fsus2   F   B♭/D   C
(Dsus2) (D)   (Dsus2) (D) (G/B)   (A)

4. Then   take ____ me dis - ap - pear - ing   through the

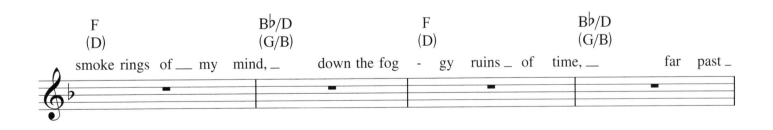

F   B♭/D   F   B♭/D
(D)   (G/B)   (D)   (G/B)

smoke rings of __ my mind, __   down the fog - gy ruins _ of time, __   far past _

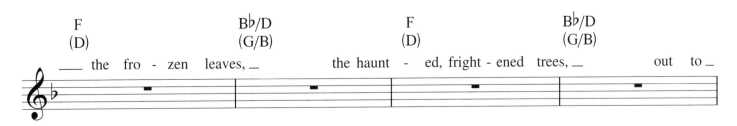

F   B♭/D   F   B♭/D
(D)   (G/B)   (D)   (G/B)

__ the fro - zen leaves, __   the haunt - ed, fright - ened trees, __   out to _

Chorus

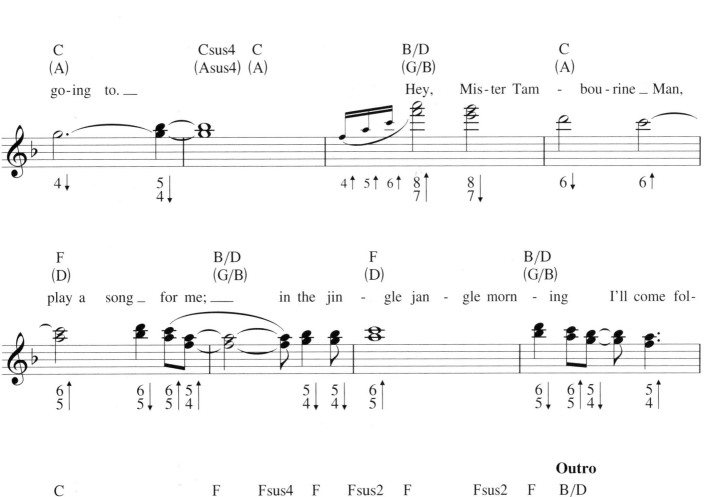

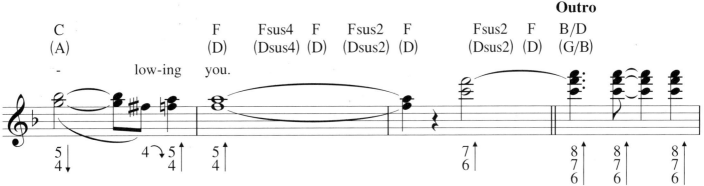

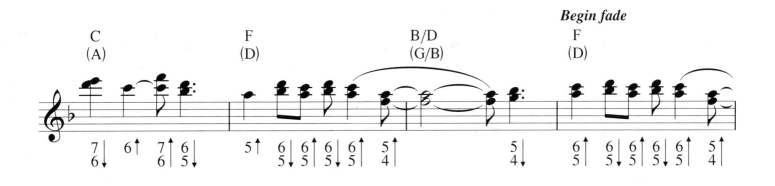

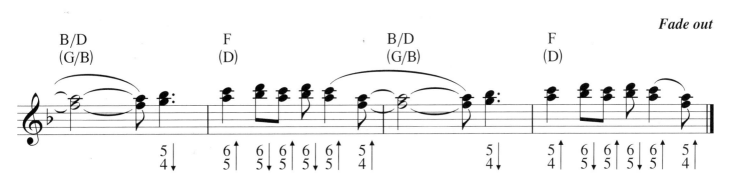

Pastures of Plenty

Words and Music by Woody Guthrie

HARMONICA

Player: Woody Guthrie
Harp Key: G Diatonic

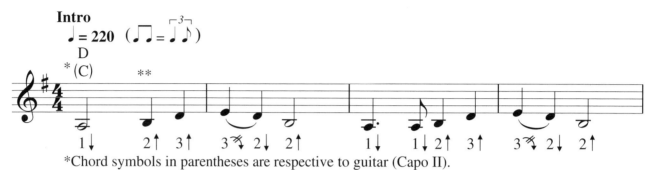

*Chord symbols in parentheses are respective to guitar (Capo II).

**Exhale through nose on blown notes
throughout for breath control.

***Throat vibrato throughout

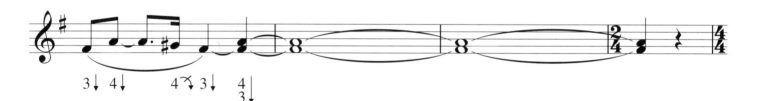

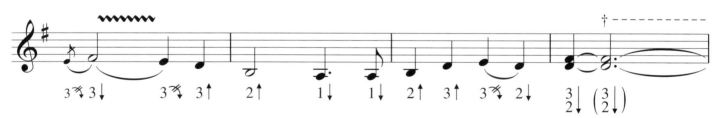

†Slight tremolo (modulate
air flow w/ tongue)

1. It's a

*Blown notes in Verses are half the volume of drawn notes.

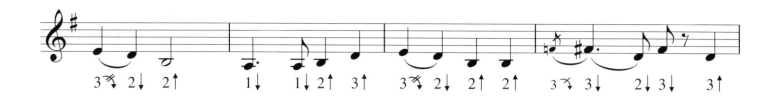

Verse
D
(C)

2. I worked in your or - chards _ of

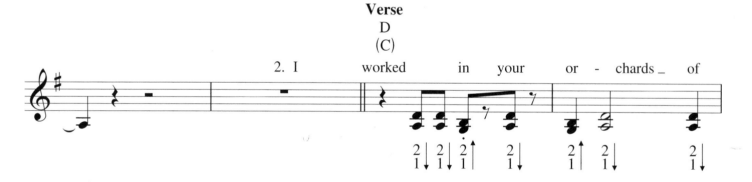

peach - es _ and prunes. Slept on the

ground _ in the light of ____ your moon. _____

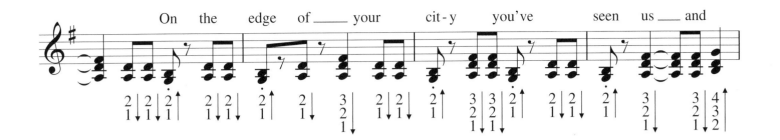

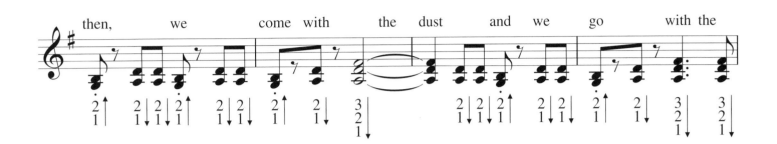

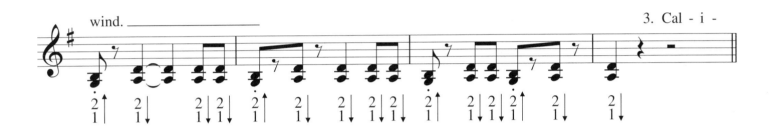

Verse
D
(C)

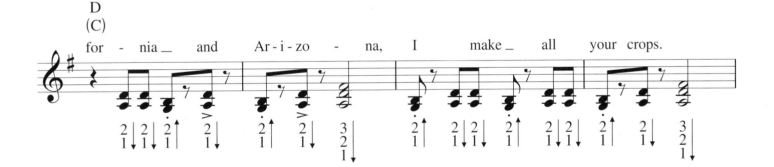

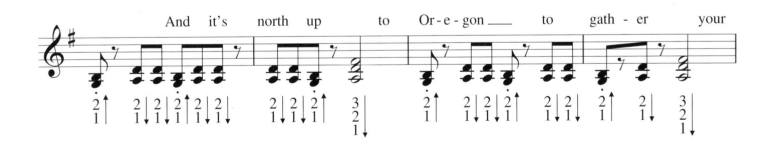

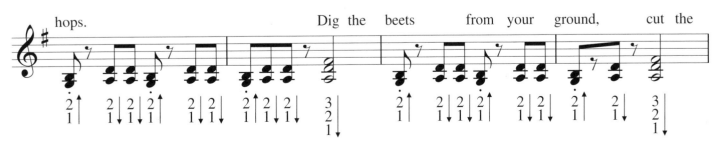

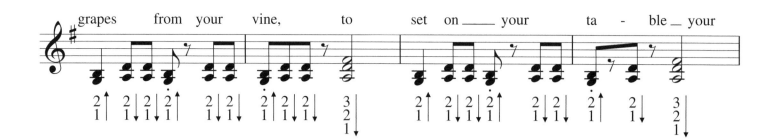

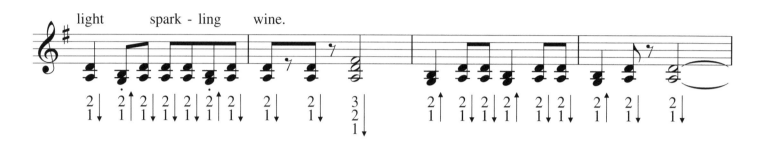

Verse
D
(C)

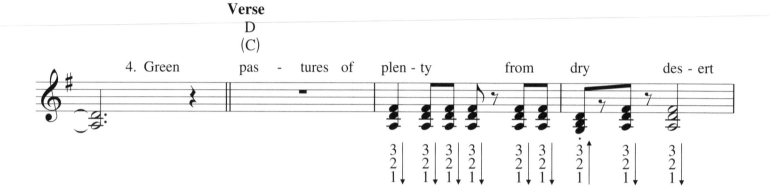

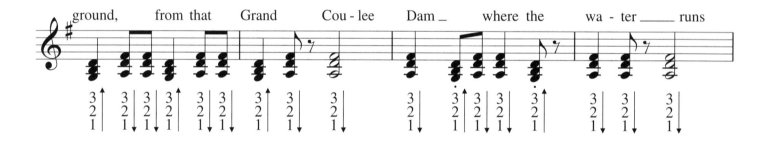

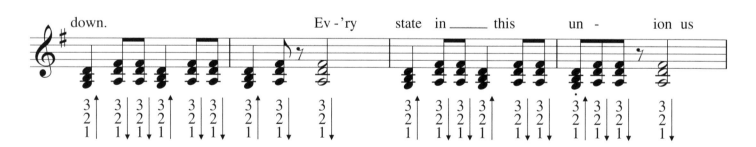

A
(G)

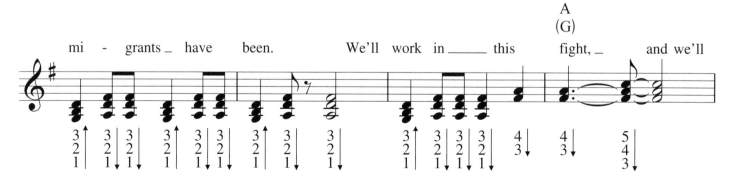

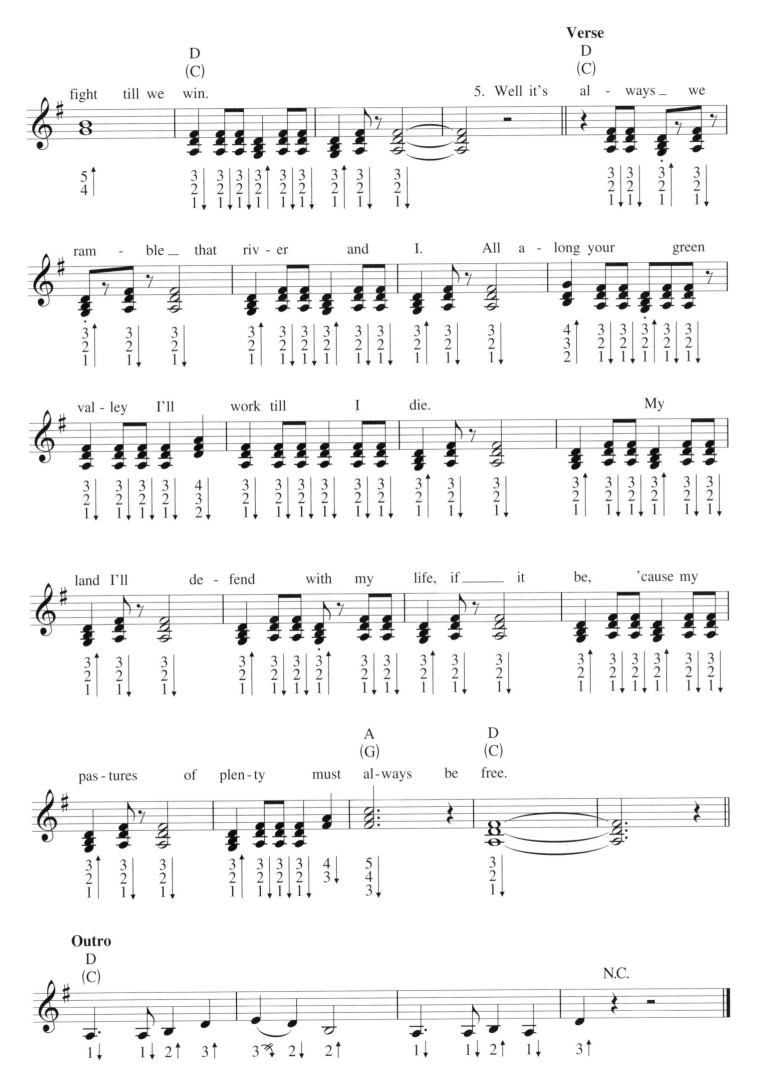

Me and Bobby McGee

Words and Music by Kris Kristofferson and Fred Foster

HARMONICA
Player: Kris Kristofferson
Harp Keys: D Diatonic
A Diatonic
E Diatonic
B Diatonic

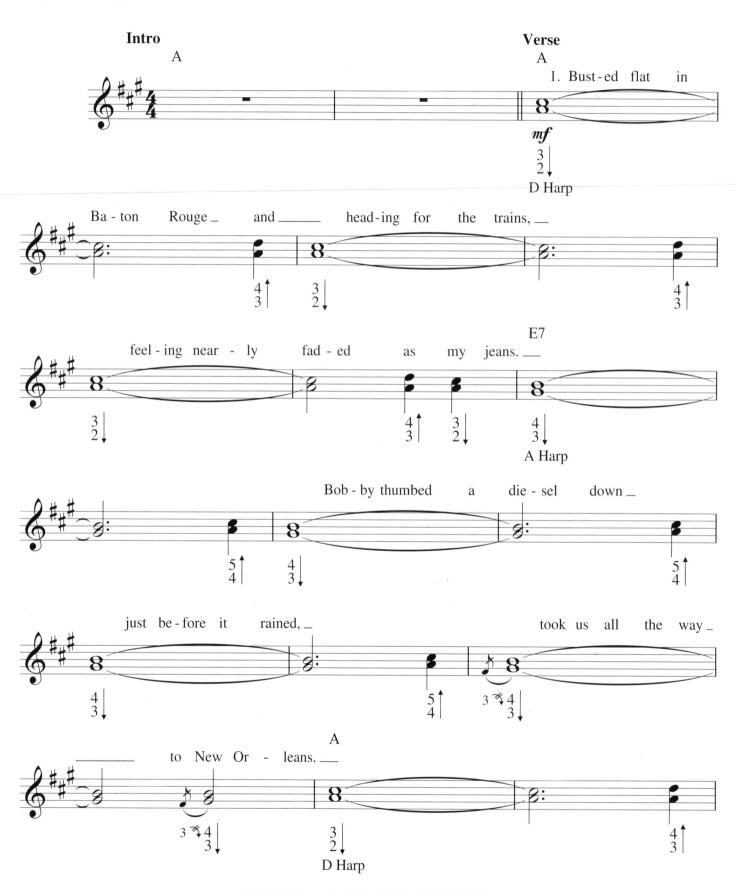

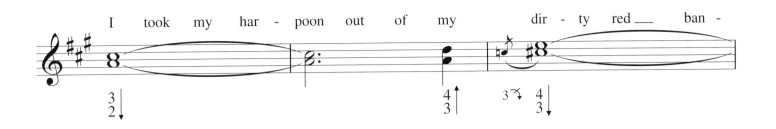

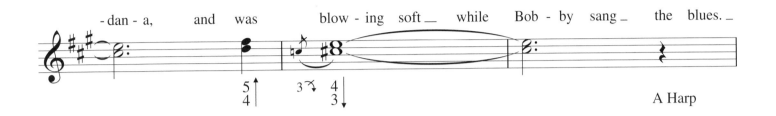

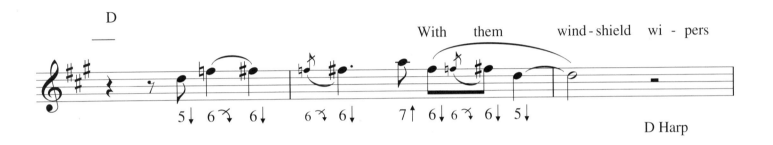

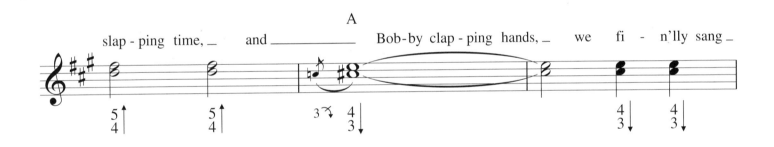

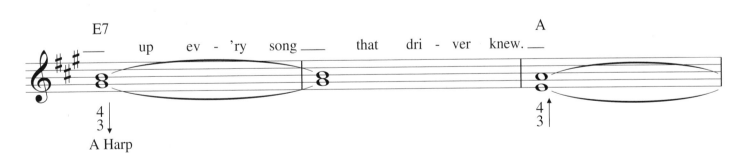

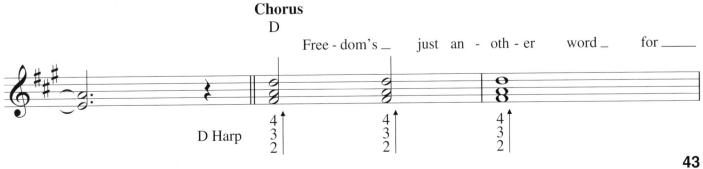

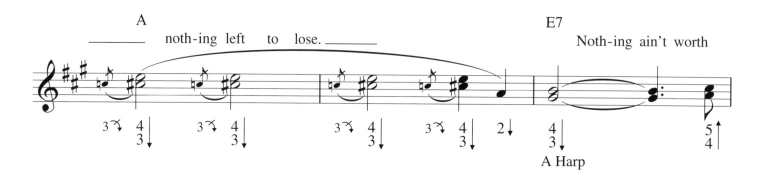

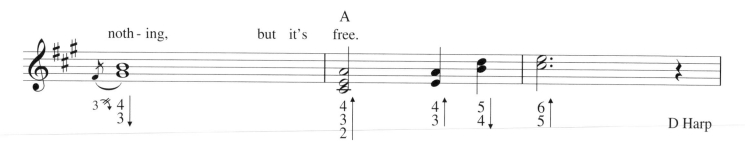

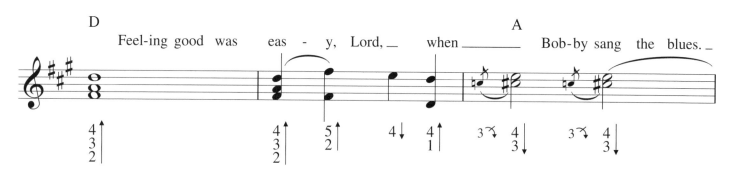

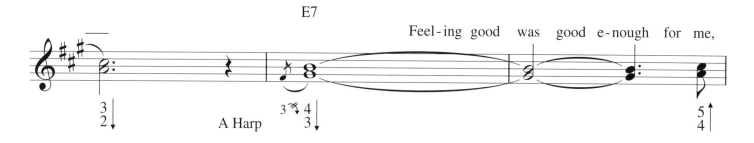

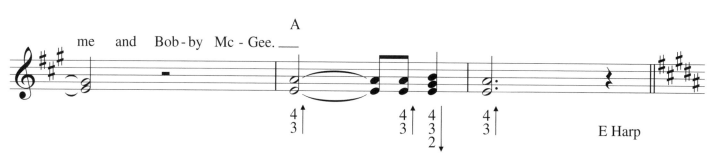

Interlude
B

Verse
B

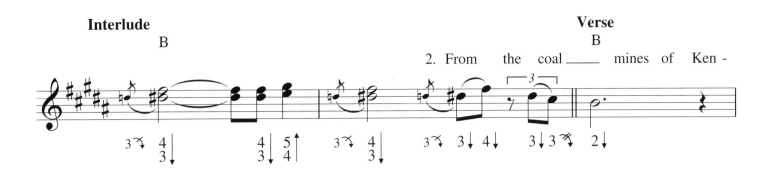

2. From the coal _____ mines of Ken -

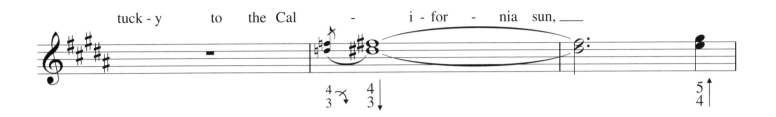

tuck - y   to the Cal - i - for - nia sun, _____

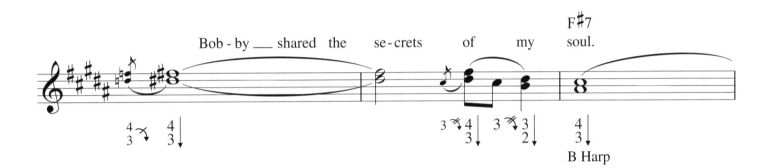

Bob - by ___ shared the se - crets of my soul.

F#7

B Harp

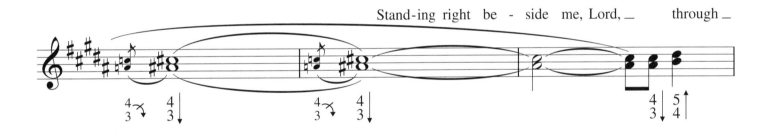

Stand-ing right be - side me, Lord, ___ through _

_____ ev -'ry-thing I'd done, _   ev -'ry night she kept _

B

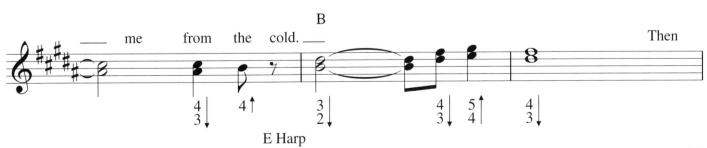

_____ me from the cold. ___   Then

E Harp

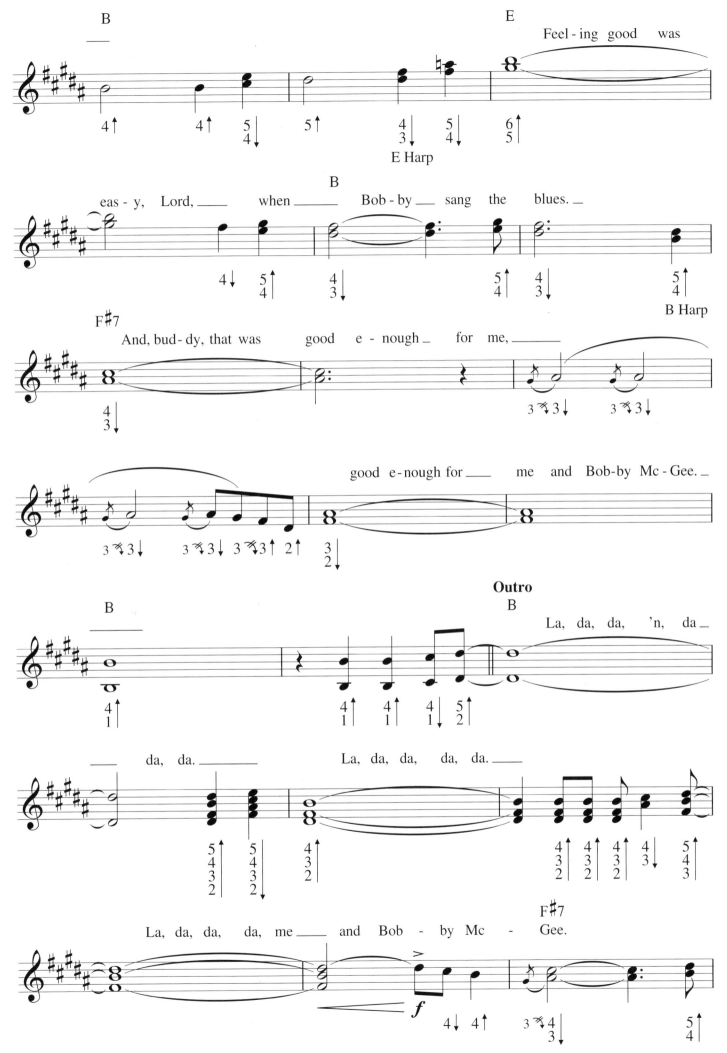

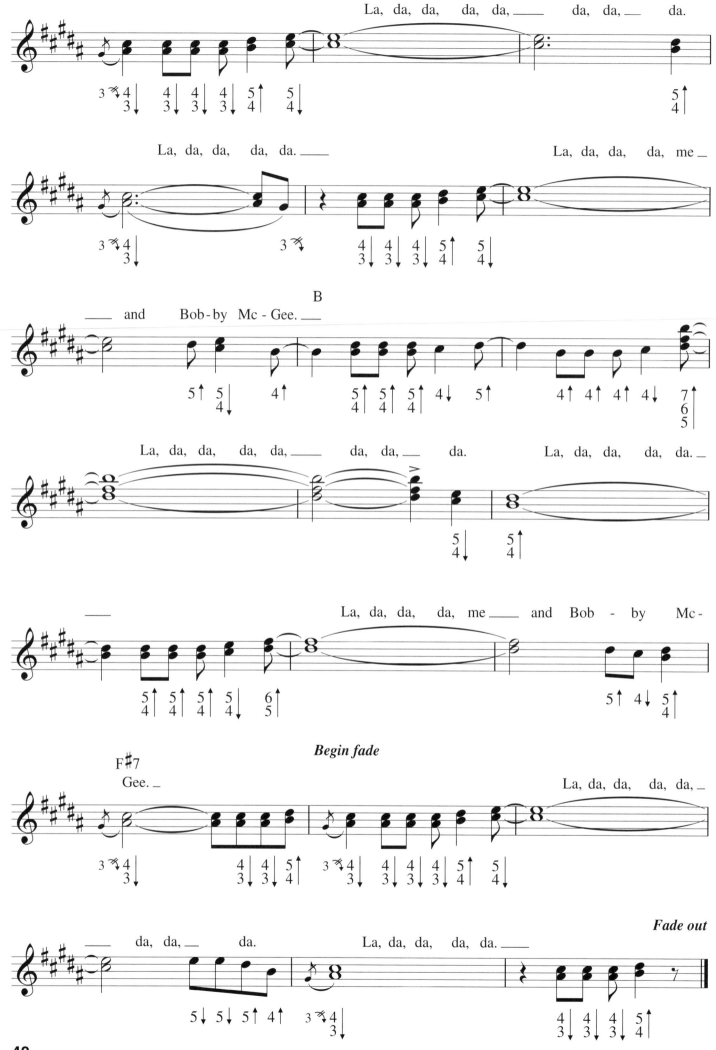